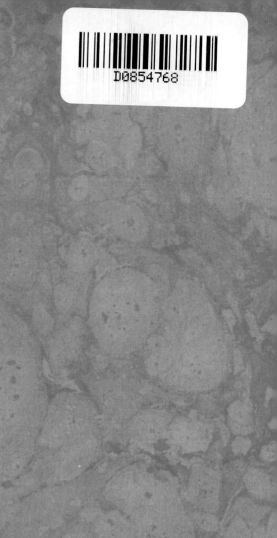

Fergus.
19ᵗ July 1998
for Godmother Andrea.

To Joseph

This edition copyright © 1997 Lion Publishing
Illustrations copyright © 1997 Danuta Mayer
Text by Mary Joslin
The author asserts the moral right
to be identified as the author of this work

Published by
Lion Publishing plc
Sandy Lane West, Oxford, England
ISBN 0 7459 3631 8

First edition 1997
10 9 8 7 6 5 4 3 2 1 0

A catalogue record for this book is available
from the British Library

Printed and bound in Spain by Bookprint

The stories and songs that inform this book about angels can be
found in the Old and New Testaments of the Bible.

Do the *Angels* watch close by?

Mary Joslin & Danuta Mayer

A LION BOOK

When the night is dark
and those who love you
are fast asleep,
are you alone with
the glow of the moon
and the raggedy clouds
and the blowing wind—
or do the angels
watch close by?

Sometimes the world seems bleak and empty.

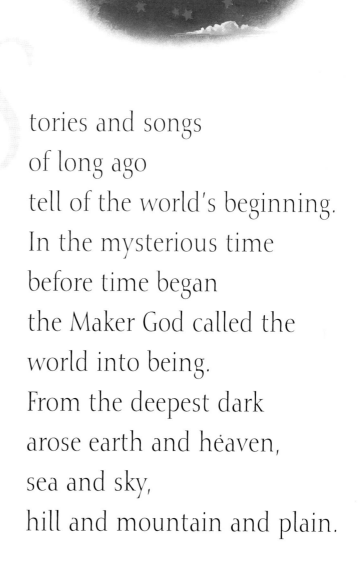

tories and songs
of long ago
tell of the world's beginning.
In the mysterious time
before time began
the Maker God called the
world into being.
From the deepest dark
arose earth and heaven,
sea and sky,
hill and mountain and plain.

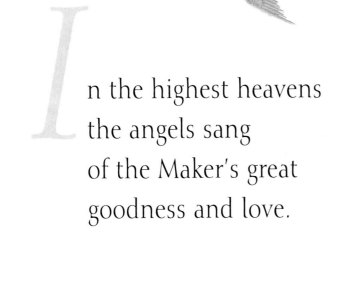

I n the highest heavens
the angels sang
of the Maker's great
goodness and love.

*Maybe the heavens
hold greater mysteries
than we imagine.*

On the world below,
the Maker God commanded
the green and growing things
to unfurl their leaves and open
their bright flowers to the sun.
As the fruit ripened in the long
summer days, the angels
rejoiced at the first harvest.

*No one knows for sure what
an angel might be.*

The world is filled with so many types of creature that no one can say what an angel might look like.

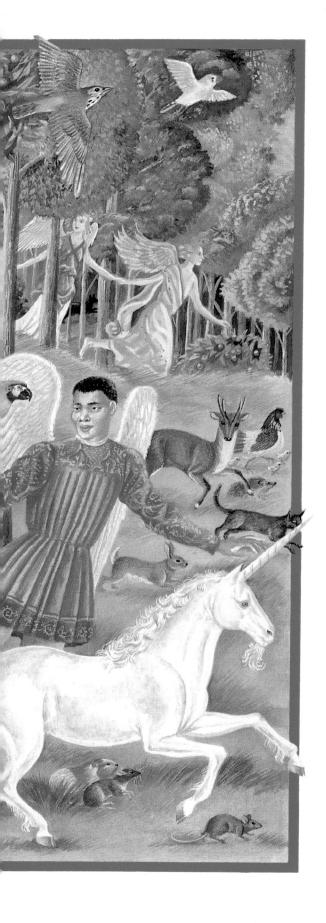

On land and
sea, the Maker God called
forth all manner of creatures:
animals of the wild lands,
animals of the farmlands,
bright birds and reptiles
and fish of every kind—
while the angels danced with
delight among them.

hen the Maker God filled the world with people, joyfully the angels joined in their songs... but the people seemed unaware.

It is easy for people to imagine that angels look like people.

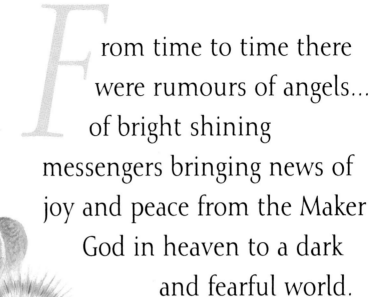

From time to time there were rumours of angels... of bright shining messengers bringing news of joy and peace from the Maker God in heaven to a dark and fearful world.

If angels come from highest heaven, perhaps they fly down on glistening wings.

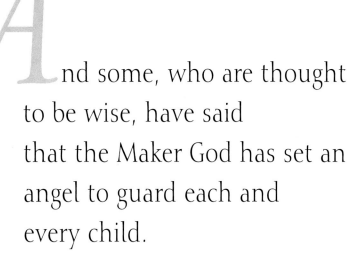

And some, who are thought to be wise, have said that the Maker God has set an angel to guard each and every child.

Can it be true that angels, all unseen, watch with infinite care over all the world?

Imagine angels walking close by, kindly and gentle and strong.

So perhaps, when night's dark shadows fall, angels enfold the fearful in a shimmering embrace.

Imagine   angels   helping   people   to   find   the   way   ahead.

W hen the world seems vast and trackless and wild, perhaps the angels show a safe path to follow.

When the world is good and kind, perhaps the angels in heaven sing together in a joyful celebration.

Imagine the angels dancing among the stars.

nd perhaps one day,
when the world is old
and the Maker God
makes all things new,
people and angels
will live together
in peace and joy and love.

*Some say that
one day, there
will be no need to
imagine angels...
for we will be
with them in a
new heaven, on a
new earth.*

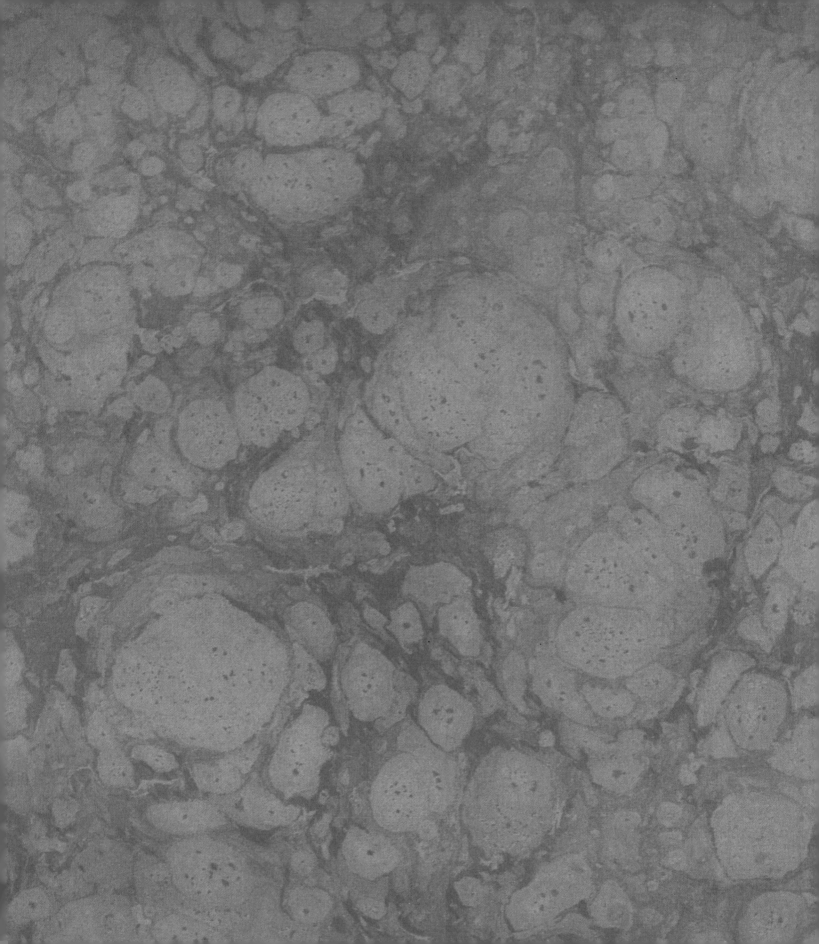